Eva's Austrian Cook Book

EVA's AUSTRIAN COOKBOOK

(C)1997-2015 Eva Thorne

All rights reserved. No part of this book may be reproduced, stored in a retrieval system, or transmitted in any form, or by any means, electronic, photocopying, mechanical recording, or otherwise, without the prior permission of the copyright owner.

First limited UK edition July 1997 published by Etcetera Press.
ISBN 0-905-119-07-X

First (EU) edition August 2006
ISBN 0-905-119-20-7

First USA edition July 2008
ISBN 978-1-4092-1794-7

3rd. USA Edition, July 2015 (pBook)
ISBN 978 –1-4637-3041-3

INTRODUCTION

Eva Thorne, back in 1984 and speaking very little English, flew to the British Channel Island of Guernsey to spend a few weeks holiday there with her restaurant owning relatives.

At a dinner party one night she met her future English husband Tony, invited that evening because he claimed to know a little German! She still is waiting to know who was that little German!

One thing led to another and a few months later they were married on Christmas Eve. They lived in Guernsey until 1989, when they moved to England, to a newly converted Old Coach House in the village of Chedzoy, Somerset. Then in 1998 they moved to their house in Austria, near Vienna.

Since her marriage, Eva has become fluent in English and while living abroad, has introduced her Viennese catering skills to local friends and neighbours, as well as to her lucky husband and his relatives. Many of the recipes in this book have been enjoyed by enthusiastic and appreciative guests, and in some cases during stays of several days at a time!

She learned to cook the traditional Viennese way from an early age, and this collection of all kinds of very tempting dishes includes some of her own creations, as well as several recipes given to her by her mother.

Page
7-9   **SOUPS & SAVOURY DISHES**
10 Rindsuppe [Beef Stock]
11 Griessnockerlsuppe [Semolina Dumpling Soup]
12 Eintropfsuppe [Drop Thickened Soup]
13 Frittatensuppe [Sliced Pancake Soup]
14 Leberknödelsuppe [Liver Dumpling Soup]
15 Gemüsesuppe [Traditional Vegetable Soup]
16 Gulaschsuppe [Hot & Spicy Beef Soup]
17 Rahmsuppe [Cream Soup]
18 Hühnersuppe [Chicken Soup]
20 Liptauer [Spicy Cheese Filling or Dip]
21 Frühlingsaufstrich [Springtime Spread]
    Knoblauch Aufstrich [Garlic and Cheese Spread]
22 Eiaufstrich [Spicy Egg Filling or Dip]
    Thunfischaufstrich [Tuna Fish Filling or Dip]
23 Hühnerleber in Schmalz [Chicken Liver in Pork Dripping]
24 Pikanter Toastwecken [Spicy Bread Loaf]

25   **MEAT DISHES**
27 Wild in Rahmsauce [Game in Cream Sauce]
28 Wienerschnitzel vom Schwein [Viennese Pork Escalope in Breadcrumbs]
29 Wiener Backhuhn [Viennese Chicken in Breadcrumbs]
30 Schweinsbraten [Viennese Pork Roast]
31 Gebratenes Huhn [Eva's Roast Chicken]
32 Faschierter Braten [Minced Meat Roast]
33 Fleischlaibchen [Minced Meat Steaks]
34 Gefüllte Paprika [Stuffed Peppers]
35 Senffleisch [Viennese Mustard Casserole]
36 Fleischstrudel [Meat & Pastry Roll]
38 Rindsgulasch [Hot & Spicy Beef Casserole]
39 Herrengulasch [Gentleman's Spicy Beef Casserole]
41 Schweinsgulasch [Hot & Spicy Pork Casserole]
42 Reisfleisch [Viennese Spicy Rice]
43 Paprikahuhn [Spicy Chicken Casserole]
44 Fleischpalatschinken [Eva's Meat Pancakes]

45 Gebratene Ente [Roast Duck]
46 Fleischtorte [Eva's Meat & Pancake Tart]
48 Fleischknödel [Meat Dumplings]

49 **VEGETABLES & OTHER SIDE DISHES**
52 Sauerkraut [Sweet & Sour White Cabbage]
53 Rotkraut [Sweet & Sour Red Cabbage]
54 Einbrenn [Special White Sauce for Vegetables]
55 Fisolen oder Grüne Bohnen [Creamed French, or Runner, Beans]
56 Kohlrüben mit Erbsen [Creamed Kohlrabi & Peas]
57 Spinat [Creamed Spinach]
58 Kohl [Creamed Cabbage]
59 Eva's Salatmarinade [Eva's Special Salad Dressing]
60 Tomatensalat [Tomato Salad]
   Fisolensalat [French Bean Salad]
61 Grüner Salat [Lettuce Salad]
   Weisser Bohnensalat [White (Butter) Bean Salad]
62 Gurkensalat [Cucumber Salad]
   Gurkensalat in Rahm [Creamed Cucumber Salad]
63 Kartoffelsalat [Potato Salad]
   Kartoffelsalat in Mayonnaise [Potato and Mayonnaise Salad]
64 Apfelkren [Apple & Horseradish Sauce]
   Semmelkren [Bread and Horseradish Sauce]
65 Fleischsalat [Meat Salad]
   Huhn in Mayonnaisesalat [Chicken in Mayonnaise Salad]
66 Kartoffel als Beilage [Recipes for Potatoes as a Side Dish]
   [Boiled Potatoes], [Simple Fried Potatoes], [Crispy Fried Potatoes], [Parsley Potatoes], [Dill Potatoes], [Mashed Potatoes]
68 Semmelknödel [Viennese Bread Roll Dumplings]
69 Kartoffelknödel [Potato Dumplings]
70 Serviettenknödel [Dumplings cooked in a Cloth]

71	**MEAT FREE DISHES**
74	Karotten und Erbsen Gemüse [Carrots & Peas]
75	Karfiol mit Butter und Brösel [Cauliflower with Butter & Breadcrumbs]
76	Geröstete Knödel [Roasted Dumplings]
77	Tomatensauce mit Knödel [Special Tomato Sauce with Dumplings]
78	Champignonsauce mit Knödel [Mushroom Sauce with Dumplings]
79	Gefüllte Melanzani [Stuffed Aubergine]
80	Kartoffelpuffer [Puffed Potato Pancakes]
81	Kartoffelgulasch [Meat free Potato Casserole]
82	Panierter Karfiol [Cauliflower in Breadcrumbs]
83	**SWEET DISHES & DESSERTS**
85	Palatschinken [Basic Pancake Recipe]
86	Topfenpalatschinken [Quark Cheese Pancakes]
87	Äpfel im Schlafrock [Apple in a Dressing Gown]
88	Kaiserschmarren [Emperor's Cut Up Pancakes]
89	Scheiterhaufen [Apple Layer Cake]
90	Marillenknödel [Apricot Dumplings]
91	**CAKES & BISCUITS**
93	Apfelkuchen [Mother's Apple Turnover]
94	Wiener Apfelstrudel [Viennese Apple Pastry]
96	Schokoladekuchen [Eva's Special Chocolate Cake]
97	Kirschenkuchen [Cherry Cake]
98	Marillenkuchen [Apricot Cake]
99	Fruchtkuchen [Fruit Cake]
100	Biskottentorte [Custard & Sponge Fingers Cake]
101	Nusskeks [Nut Biscuits]
102	Husarenbusserln [Hussar's Kisses]
103	Marzipanpilze [Marzipan Mushrooms]
104	Rumkugeln [Rum Balls]
105	Topfenteigpolsterln [Quark Pastry Pillows]
106	Vanillekipferln [Vanilla Crescent Biscuits]

Soups & Savoury Dishes

NOTES

Introducing SOUP DISHES

In Austria, soups are usually served as a starter to a lunch-time meal. Hot, thin soups are considered excellent for the digestion of what is to come later!

Thin, consommé type, soups were traditionally made with fresh beef and vegetable ingredients. Nowadays, they are often made with beef stock cubes.

Vegetable Soup followed by a sweet dish was the traditional lunch time meal in our Catholic country on a Friday, as meat was never allowed.

In earlier times, helpings of thick soup with bread were often considered sufficient for a complete meal.

About SAVOURY DISHES

If you ask for a sandwich in Vienna, you will always get an open one, made from a slice of crusty white bread, with a special topping.

Recipes for toppings can always be used for fillings in double-sided English style sandwiches. Also as dips with toast fingers, or any kind of unsweetened biscuits.

RINDSUPPE [Consommé or Bouillon Beef Stock Soup, Traditional Recipe]

Ingredients:
- 18 ozs. stewing steak
- 18 ozs. beef bones, sawn into pieces
- 2 large carrots
- 2 medium turnips
- 1 medium onion
- 1 small bunch of parsley
- 1 teaspoon of black peppercorns
- 1 teaspoon of salt

Procedure: Peel the vegetables. Boil the bones for 5 mins then drain off the water. Rinse the bones in cold water. Pour 2 pints of water into a deep saucepan. Tip in the meat and bones and bring to the boil. Simmer for one hour, uncovered.

Add the rest of the ingredients and bring back to the boil. Simmer for a further hour then drain off the stock into a separate container. The remaining meat can be separated from the bones and used as an ingredient in a meat salad (see page 65).

The quicker, modern recipe:-
Ingredients:
- 2 beef stock cubes
- 1 large carrot, peeled and very thinly sliced
- ¼ teaspoon of caraway seeds
- ¼ teaspoon of dried thyme

Procedure: Bring the ingredients to boil in 2 pints of water and cook for 15 minutes to complete the stock.

Note: The above alternatives, provide a consommé type stock to which various other ingredients are added to make the special soups described in the following pages.

GRIESSNOCKERLSUPPE
[Semolina Dumplings Soup]

Ingredients:
    2 pints of beef stock, as previously prepared
    1¼ ozs. of salted butter
    1 egg
    2½ ozs. semolina
    a sprinkling of ground nutmeg

Procedure:
    Whisk the butter and egg together in a bowl.
    Add the semolina and the nutmeg.
    Mix thoroughly into a paste to become the dumpling mixture. Leave in the refrigerator for 15 minutes.

    Bring the soup stock to boil in a saucepan.

    Dip a tablespoon into the hot soup to wet it, then use it to scoop up some of the mixture from the bowl. Gently shake off the first dumpling into the soup, allowing the spoon to become wet again.

    Repeat this procedure until all the paste mixture is used up, forming 8 dumplings.

    Bring the soup back to the boil. Cover the saucepan with a lid and simmer for 7 minutes. Remove it from the heat, then lift the lid and pour in a tablespoon of cold water. Replace the lid and leave for 10 minutes to allow the dumplings to rise.

Serving:
    Serve with 2 dumplings per bowl of soup and optionally sprinkle some chopped chives over them.

EINTROPFSUPPE
[Drop Thickened Soup]

Ingredients:
    2 pints stock, as previously prepared
    1 egg
    2 ozs. plain flour
    2 tablespoons of cold water

Procedure:
    Mix the flour, egg, and water together, preferably in a suitable jug.

    Bring the soup stock to boil in a saucepan.

    Slowly pour the mixture into the soup, stirring continuously as it thickens.

    Simmer for 5 minutes.

Serving:
    Serve optionally with some chopped chives or parsley, sprinkled on top of the soup.

FRITTATENSUPPE
[Sliced Pancake soup]

Ingredients:

    2 pints beef stock, as previously prepared
    1 egg
    3½ ozs plain flour
    ½ pint milk
    a sprinkling of salt

Procedure:

    Mix the flour, egg, milk and salt together in a suitable jug.

    Heat some cooking oil in a frying pan and make the mixture into thin pancakes. While still hot, roll up each pancake and then allow them to cool.

    Bring the soup stock to boil in a saucepan.

    Slice the pancake rolls into thin coils and drop them into the boiling soup. Remove from the heat.

Serving:

    Serve optionally with some chopped chives or parsley, sprinkled over the soup.

LEBERKNÖDELSUPPE
[Liver Dumplings Soup]

Ingredients:

2 pints stock, as previously prepared
5½ ozs. minced pig's liver
1 Viennese bread roll
1 oz. salted butter
1 egg
1½ ozs. breadcrumbs
1 small onion
a sprinkling of black pepper, salt and dried marjoram

Procedure:

Place the bread rolls in cold water until they are fully soaked. Squeeze out the surplus liquid from the rolls and place them into a bowl.

Finely chop the onion and glaze it with the butter in a frying pan. Place the liver, egg, onion and the rest of the ingredients into the bowl and mix thoroughly into a firm paste.

Place the bowl into the refrigerator for 15 minutes.

Bring the soup stock to the boil in a suitable saucepan.

Dip your hands into some cold water and then form the mixture into 8 small balls. Drop them into the boiling soup, then bring it back to the boil and simmer for 15 minutes.

Serving:

Serve optionally with some chopped chives or parsley, sprinkled over the soup.

GEMÜSESUPPE
[Traditional Vegetable Soup]

Ingredients:
- 4 large carrots
- 1 large parsnip
- 3½ ozs. peas
- 3½ ozs. stringless green beans
- 1 large potato
- 1 vegetable stock cube
- 2 ozs. salted butter
- 1 tablespoon plain flour
- a sprinkling of black pepper and salt

Procedure:

Peel and dice the vegetables, and add to the vegetable stock cube in a saucepan containing 2 pints of water and bring to the boil.

Lightly brown the flour in the butter in a pan. Remove from the heat, add 1 tablespoon of cold water and stir well to make a smooth white sauce.

When the vegetables are ready, pour them, with the stock, into the pan with the white sauce.

Boil until the soup thickens, then add the pepper and the salt.

GULASCHSUPPE
[Hot and Spicy Beef Soup]

Ingredients:

    11 ozs. stewing steak, or beef shin, cut into small pieces
    1 medium onion
    2 teaspoons of powdered sweet paprika
    2 teaspoons of caraway seeds
    1 teaspoon of dried marjoram
    ½ teaspoon of black pepper
    a sprinkling of salt
    1 large potato
    1 beef stock cube
    2 Frankfurter sausages
    2 tablespoons cooking oil

Procedure:

    Peel and dice the onion, and glaze in the cooking oil.

    Pour 2 pints of water into a saucepan with all the ingredients except the potato and sausages, and boil for an hour.

    Peel and dice the potato and add it to the soup. Simmer for another 30 minutes, then slice the sausages into small pieces and add to the soup, ready to serve.

    If preferred, the soup can be thickened by adding a little pre-mixed flour and water, or any suitable thickening agent.

RAHMSUPPE
[Cream Soup]

Ingredients, serves 2:

    1 pint soured cream, or créme fraiche
    1 beef stock cube
    2 teaspoons of chopped parsley
    1 large potato
    a sprinkling of black pepper
    a sprinkling of powdered nutmeg

Procedure:

    Boil the potato, then peel and slice it.

    Pour the soured cream into a saucepan. If you use creme fraiche, add a little milk to thin it.

    Add the beef stock cube and the potato slices with the rest of the ingredients.
    Heat gently, ready to serve.

Serving:

    Serve with a slice of brown bread toast.

HÜHNERSUPPE
[Chicken Soup]

Ingredients, serves 4:
Soup:
- 4 chicken legs
- 1 chicken stock cube
- 2 tablespoons of chopped parsley
- 2 large carrots
- 1 medium onion
- a sprinkling of salt
- a sprinkling of black pepper

Dumplings:
- 2 Viennese bread rolls
- 1 egg
- 1 tablespoon of cooking oil
- 4 tablespoons of breadcrumbs
- a sprinkling of salt and dried thyme

Procedure:

Roughly bone the chicken legs.

Peel the carrots. Pour 2 pints of water into a saucepan then add the chicken and bones. Add the rest of the ingredients except the parsley.

Bring to the boil and simmer for an hour.

Meanwhile, soak the bread rolls in water then squeeze out the surplus, and place them into a mixing bowl with the rest of the dumplings' ingredients.

Mix well into a paste and store in the refrigerator until required.

When ready, sieve the soup into another saucepan. Empty the sieve on to a cutting board and discard the chicken skin, the bones and residual onion pieces. Cut up the chicken meat and carrots into small pieces and add them to the soup.

Thicken the soup with a little pre-mixed flour and milk, or any suitable thickening agent. Add the chopped parsley.

Bring the soup to the boil again, then quickly form the dumpling paste into 8 little balls and add them to the soup.

Simmer for 10 minutes, ready to serve.

LIPTAUER
[Spicy Cheese Filling, or Dip]

Ingredients:

    9 ozs. Gervaise or Philadelphia cheese
    4 ozs. salted butter
    1 small onion, finely chopped
    1 medium sized pickled cucumber, finely chopped
    1 segment from a garlic clove, finely chopped
    1 teaspoon of French mustard
    1 teaspoon of powdered paprika
    5 pickled capers, finely chopped
    1 teaspoon of caraway seeds
    a dash of Worcestershire sauce
    a sprinkling of black pepper, or cayenne pepper if preferred really hot.

Procedure:

    Mix the ingredients well together. For best results leave the mixture overnight in the refrigerator, before use.

FRÜHLINGS AUFSTRICH
[Springtime Spread]

Ingredients:
- 9 ozs. Philadelphia cream cheese (or similar)
- ½ red pepper, finely chopped
- 2 tablespoons of chives, finely chopped
- 1 tablespoon of parsley, finely chopped
- a sprinkling of salt and pepper to taste

Procedure:
Mix all the ingredients together.

Serving:
Serve with brown bread.
Can also be used as a filling for stuffed tomatoes.

KNOBLAUCH AUFSTRICH
[Garlic and Cheese Spread]

Ingredients:
- 9 ozs. Philadelphia cream cheese (or similar)
- 3 cloves of garlic, crushed.
- 1 tablespoon of garlic chives, finely chopped (optional)
- a sprinkling of salt

Procedure:
Mix everything together.

Serving:
Serve with toasted brown bread.

EIAUFSTRICH
[Spicy egg filling, or dip]

Ingredients:

    5 hard boiled eggs
    2 tablespoons of mayonnaise
    1 small onion
    1 teaspoon of French mustard
    1 teaspoon of curry powder
    a dash of Worcestershire sauce
    a sprinkling of salt

Procedure:
    Peel and finely chop the onion.
    Shell and finely chop the eggs.

    Mix the ingredients well together.

THUNFISCHAUFSTRICH
[Tuna Fish Filling or Dip]

Ingredients:
    1 tin of tuna, in brine
    1 hard-boiled egg
    2 tablespoons of mayonnaise
    1 pickled cucumber, finely chopped
    a sprinkling of black pepper

Procedure:
    Drain off the brine from the tuna.
    Shell and finely chop the egg.

    Mix the ingredients well together.

HÜHNERLEBER IN SCHMALZ
[Chicken Liver in Pork Dripping]

Ingredients:

    9 ozs. chicken liver
    9 ozs. pork dripping
    1 segment from a garlic clove
    a sprinkling of salt and pepper

Procedure:
    Melt the dripping in a frying pan on a very low heat. Add the garlic and brown it to give taste to the dripping. Discard the garlic.

    Thinly slice the chicken liver and gently fry it in the dripping until cooked through.

    When ready, remove the pan from the heat and sprinkle in the salt and pepper.

    Pour the mixture into a suitable, preferably glazed earthenware, dish to cool and set hard.

Serving:
    Best served spread over sliced dark brown bread.

PIKANTER TOASTWECKEN
[Spicy Bread Loaf]

Ingredients, serves 6-8:

    1 white sandwich loaf, unsliced

Filling:
- 9 ozs. mayonnaise, (low fat if preferred)
- 2 tablespoons French mustard
- 3 hard-boiled eggs, finely chopped
- 11 ozs. continental spiced sausage, or similar, chopped into small cubes
- 11 ozs. Cheddar cheese, or similar, chopped into small cubes
- 5 pickled cucumbers, finely chopped
- 1 generous sprinkling of Worcestershire sauce
- 1 generous sprinkling of black pepper

Procedure:

    Cut the loaf of bread, in the middle, into two equal end pieces. Scoop out each soft interior, leaving two shells having walls about half an inch thick.

    Put the filling ingredients into a large bowl. Add the removed part of the bread and mix all well together.

    Stuff the two half shells with the filling, pressing it in firmly.

    Place the two halves of the loaf together again and wrap them inside a large sheet of aluminium foil.
    Leave overnight in the refrigerator.

Serving:

    When ready, cut thin slices from the Loaf and serve.

Meat Dishes

NOTES

WILD IN RAHMSAUCE
[Game in Cream Sauce]

Ingredients, serves 4:
  35 ozs. of venison, or rabbit
  1 large carrot
  1 medium turnip
  1 small onion
  2 ozs. streaky bacon
  1 small bunch of parsley
  1 teaspoon of dried juniper berries
  3 bay leaves
  1 teaspoon of black peppercorns
  1 teaspoon of salt
  1 pint of red wine
  2 tablespoons of brandy
  1 medium sized jar of cranberry sauce
  2 digestive biscuits
  2 tablespoons of soured cream or créme fraiche

Procedure:
  Place the meat and wine in a large oven dish which has a lid. Peel and slice the vegetables and lay them around the meat with the bacon and the rest of the ingredients except the brandy, cranberry sauce, the biscuits and cream.
  Put on the lid, and oven cook at 360°F (180°C) for 2 hours.

  Remove the meat to a cutting board and slice it into medium sized pieces. Discard the onion and bay leaves. Pour off the gravy into a blender with the biscuit, 2 tablespoons of cranberry sauce and the brandy. Blend gently, then pour the gravy back into the oven dish.
  Gently mix in the cream, then put the meat back in and continue cooking in the oven for another 2 to 3 minutes.

Serving:
  Best served with Servicttenknödel (page 70) and slices of orange decorated with the rest of the cranberry sauce.

WIENERSCHNITZEL VOM SCHWEIN
[Viennese Pork Escalope in Breadcrumbs]

If you order Wienerschnitzel in a restaurant, it should be veal, but at home most Austrians use this more tasty, and economical, recipe!

Ingredients, serves 2:
- 2 pork meat slices, very thin (escalopes)
- 1 egg
- 4 tablespoons of plain flour, not self-raising
- 4 tablespoons of dried golden breadcrumbs
- a sprinkling of salt
- 1¼ cups cooking oil

Procedure:

Take 2 dinner plates and a large soup plate. Put the flour on one dinner plate, and the breadcrumbs on the other. Break the egg into 1 tablespoon of water in the soup plate and stir together. Put the meat on to a cutting board and cover it with a sheet of thin plastic material. Reduce its thickness, by gently hammering on top of the plastic sheet, so as not to damage the meat.

Sprinkle salt on each side. Gently wipe the first pork escalope into the plate of flour, both sides. Then into the egg mixture, both sides. Next, press it into the plate of breadcrumbs, both sides, making sure the coating is even all over. Place the breaded meat on to a dry board, then repeat the procedure with the second escalope. Rapidly, heat up the oil in a suitable pan to become very hot. Carefully slide the two schnitzels in the hot oil and leave for 1 minute. Turn them over to seal, then fry them for 5 minutes on each side.

Serving:

With a slice of fresh lemon, dill or parsley potatoes and a mixed salad. Alternatively, served only with potato salad. See page 63 in the Side Dishes section.

WIENER BACKHUHN
[Viennese Chicken in Breadcrumbs]

Ingredients, serves 2:
- 2 chicken legs, skinned if preferred.
- 1 large egg
- 8 tablespoons of plain flour, self-raising is not suitable
- 8 tablespoons of dry golden breadcrumbs
- a sprinkling of salt
- 1¼ pints cooking oil

Procedure:

Take 2 dinner plates and one large soup plate. Put the plain flour on one dinner plate and the breadcrumbs on the other. Break the egg into 1 tablespoon of water in the soup plate and stir together.

Salt the chicken legs.
Turn the first chicken leg around in the plate of flour until completely covered. Similarly next into the plate of egg mixture. Finally press and turn it into the plate of breadcrumbs, making sure the coating is pressed in and spread evenly.

Place the first breaded leg on to a dried cutting board then repeat the procedure with the second one.

Rapidly, heat up the oil in a suitable frying pan to become medium hot. Carefully slide the two legs into the hot oil and leave for one minute. Turn them over and over to seal and then fry them gently for 50 minutes, occasionally turning them over.

Serving:

Serve with a slice of fresh lemon, plain fried potatoes and mixed salad.

SCHWEINSBRATEN
[Viennese Pork Roast]

Ingredients, serves 4:
Roast:
- 35 ozs. pork chops meat, boned and rolled with the skin left on for the crackling.
- 2 crushed garlic cloves
- 2 teaspoons of caraway seeds
- 1 teaspoon of salt

Gravy:
- ½ pint water
- 1 garlic clove
- 1 medium onion

Basting:
- ½ cup cold salted water

Procedure:

Place the meat into a roasting dish and sprinkle over the crushed garlic, caraway seeds and salt. Peel the garlic clove and the onion and place them in the side of the roasting dish with the half pint of water to start the gravy.

Heat the oven to 430°F (220°C) and put in the baking dish with its lid on. Immediately turn down the oven to 395°F (200°C) and cook for 1 hour.

Open the oven door and remove the lid from the baking dish. Roast for a further 40 minutes, basting the cold salted water over the meat, at frequent intervals, to crisp up the crackling and make up the gravy. Leave for a few minutes before serving.

Serving:

Best served with sauerkraut and Viennese bread dumplings. Alternatively it can be served with rice. See the Side Dishes section.

GEBRATENES HUHN
[Eva's Roast Chicken]

Ingredients, serves 4:
- 1 medium sized chicken
- 1 medium sized onion
- 1 sprinkling of dried thyme
- 1 tablespoon of French mustard
- 2 tablespoons of salted butter
- 1 chicken stock cube
- ½ cup cold salted water
- 2 medium sized, peeled apples.

Procedure:

Mix the butter, thyme, mustard and chicken stock cube, well together in a small bowl.

Stuff the chicken with the apples then place it in a roasting dish. Brush the butter and mustard mixture over it. Peel the onion and put it in the dish beside the chicken, with a few tablespoons of plain water to make the gravy later.

Place the dish in the oven and roast for 75 minutes at 395°F (200°C). Brush cold salted water over the chicken every 10 to 15 minutes to crisp its skin and to continue to make up the gravy.

When ready, discard the onion and drain off the gravy into a suitable jug.

Serving:

This dish should be served with rice and a mixed salad. See the Side Dishes section.

FASCHIERTER BRATEN
[Minced Meat Roast]

Ingredients, serves 4:

- 18 ozs. lean minced pork
- 1½ Viennese bread rolls
- 1 medium onion
- 3 tablespoons of cooking oil
- 1 egg
- 3½ ozs. breadcrumbs
- 1 teaspoon of salt
- 1 tablespoon of French mustard
- 1 teaspoon of dried marjoram
- a sprinkling of black pepper
- a sprinkling of dried thyme
- a dash of Worcestershire sauce

Procedure:

Soak the bread rolls in water and squeeze out the surplus liquid.

Peel and slice the onion, into a frying pan, and glaze it in some heated oil.

Mix together the meat, bread rolls, the onion, and The rest of the ingredients. Leave the mixture for 30 minutes.

Form the mixture into the shape of a loaf and place it in a deep, greased, baking dish. Spread a little butter over the mixture then bake for 45 minutes at 395°F (200°), or until the top is nicely browned.

Serving:

Best served hot from the oven with mashed potato and vegetables, and gravy as preferred.

FLEISCHLAIBCHEN
[Minced Meat Steaks]

Ingredients, serves 4:

    18 ozs. lean minced pork, or beef
    1½ Vienna bread rolls
    1 medium onion
    3 tablespoons cooking oil
    1 egg
    7 ozs. dry golden breadcrumbs
    1 teaspoon of salt
    1 tablespoon of French mustard
    1 teaspoon of dried marjoram
    a sprinkling of black pepper
    a sprinkling of dried thyme
    a dash of Worcestershire sauce

Procedure:
    Soak the bread rolls in water and squeeze out the surplus liquid.

    Peel and slice the onion and glaze it in heated oil.
    Mix together the meat, bread rolls, the onion, and half the breadcrumbs with the rest of the ingredients.
    Leave the mixture for 30 minutes.

    Form the mixture into 4 balls then roll them, in turn, in the rest of the breadcrumbs. Press down each ball of mixture down to form them into thick steaks then fry in hot oil for about 18 minutes turning them halfway through to make both sides crispy.

Serving:
    Best served hot from the pan with mashed potato and vegetables, or salad, or as preferred. My husband refers to these tasty items as Austrian Hamburgers ..!

GEFÜLLTE PAPRIKA
[Stuffed Peppers]

Ingredients, serves 4:
Filling:
- 10 ozs. lean minced pork
- 1 Viennese bread roll
- 1 medium onion
- 2 tablespoons of cooking oil
- 1 egg
- 2 ozs. breadcrumbs
- 1 teaspoon of salt
- 1 tablespoon of French mustard
- 1 teaspoon of dried marjoram
- 4 green peppers
- a sprinkling of black pepper
- a sprinkling of dried thyme
- a dash of Worcestershire sauce

Sauce:
- 2 tins of thick tomato soup
- 2 tablespoons of sugar
- a sprinkling of cayenne pepper (optional)

Procedure:
Soak the bread roll in water and squeeze out the surplus liquid. Peel and slice the onion and glaze it in heated oil. Mix together the meat, bread roll, the onion, the egg and the rest of the filling ingredients. Mix in the breadcrumbs, then leave the mixture for 30 minutes. Remove the top and the seeds from the peppers then stuff them with the meat mixture. Replace the tops of the peppers, secured with wooden cocktail sticks. Mix the sauce ingredients together in a suitable jug then pour them into a baking casserole. Place in the peppers then bake at 395° F (200°C) for 45 minutes.

Serving:
Best served with rice.

SENFFLEISCH
[Viennese Mustard Casserole]

Ingredients, serves 2:

    18 ozs. pork meat cut into medium sized pieces
    7 ozs. onions
    1 tablespoon of dried marjoram
    1 teaspoon of black pepper
    1 teaspoon of salt
    2 tablespoons of French mustard
    4 tablespoons cooking oil

Procedure:

    Peel and dice the onion, and brown in the cooking oil in a saucepan. Pour in half a pint of water and boil for 15 minutes.

    Add the meat and the rest of the ingredients. Simmer for about 50 minutes.

    Thicken by adding a little pre-mixed flour and water, or any suitable thickening agent.

Serving:

    This dish should be served with creamy mashed potatoes or rice. See the Side Dishes section.

FLEISCHSTRUDEL
[Meat Roll in Pastry]

Ingredients, serves 6-8 as part of a party buffet:

    1 sheet of pre-prepared, frozen, puff pastry
    18 ozs. lean minced pork or turkey
    1 Viennese bread roll
    1 medium onion
    3 tablespoons of cooking oil
    1 egg
    1 small tin of sliced carrots
    4 tablespoons of breadcrumbs
    1 tablespoon of French mustard
    2 tablespoons of chopped chives
    a sprinkling of salt and black pepper
    a dash of Worcestershire sauce

Procedure:

    Unwrap the pre-prepared puff pastry and allow it to defrost, as recommended on the pack.

    Soak the bread rolls in water and squeeze out the surplus liquid.

    Peel and slice the onion and glaze it in the heated oil.

    Mix together the meat, bread rolls, the onion, and the rest of ingredients. Leave the mixture for 30 minutes.

    Meanwhile, roll out the puff pastry to about 12 x 12 inches square.

    Lay the mixture along the centre of the pastry and shape it into a shallow loaf. Fold the pastry over to overlap in the middle.

Press the ends down to seal in the mixture and then place the 'strudel' on to a greased baking tray.

Brush over the pastry with some milk then bake for 45 minutes at 395°F (200°C).

Serving:
Can be served cold as part of a buffet, or warm with salad or vegetables, as a main meal for 4 persons.

RINDSGULASCH
[Hot and Spicy Beef Casserole]

Ingredients, serves 2:

    18 ozs. stewing steak, or beef shin, cut into medium sized pieces
    14 ozs. onions
    2 teaspoons powdered sweet paprika
    1 teaspoons caraway seeds
    1 teaspoon of dried marjoram
    1 teaspoon of black pepper
    1 teaspoon of salt
    ½ teaspoon of garlic salt
    a dash of cayenne pepper if preferred very hot
    1 beef stock cube
    4 tablespoons cooking oil

Procedure:

    Peel and dice the onion, and brown in the cooking oil in a saucepan. Pour in a pint of water and boil for 17 minutes. Remove from the heat then pour in a dash of cold water with the rest of the ingredients, except the meat.

    Warning! Never put sweet paprika directly into hot oil, as this can make it taste very bitter!

    Stir well, then add the meat. Simmer for 2 hours. Goulasch should be thickened by adding a little pre-mixed flour and water, or any suitable thickening agent.

Serving:

    This dish should be served with boiled potatoes. See the Side Dishes section.

HERRENGULASCH
[Gentleman's Spicy Beef Casserole]

Ingredients, serves 2:
- 18 ozs. stewing steak, or beef shin, cut into medium sized pieces
- 14 ozs. onions
- 2 teaspoons of powdered sweet paprika
- 1 teaspoon of caraway seeds
- 1 teaspoon of dried marjoram
- 1 teaspoon of black pepper
- ½ teaspoon of salt
- ½ teaspoon of garlic salt
- a sprinkling of cayenne pepper, only if preferred very hot!
- 1 beef stock cube
- 4 tablespoons of cooking oil

Procedure:

Peel and dice the onion, and brown in the cooking oil in a saucepan. Pour in a pint of water and boil for 17 minutes. Remove from the heat then pour in a dash of cold water with the rest of the ingredients, except the meat.

Warning! Never put sweet paprika directly into hot oil as this can make it taste very bitter.

Stir well, then add the meat. Simmer for 2 hours. Goulash should be thickened by adding a little pre-mixed flour and water, or any suitable thickening agent.

Serving:

Gentleman's Goulash should be served with a boiled Frankfurter sausage, a fried egg, and a pickled cucumber; plus boiled potatoes. See the Side Dishes section.

KARTOFFELGULASCH
[Viennese Hot and Spicy Potato Casserole]

Ingredients:
- 18 ozs. potatoes, cut into small pieces
- 14 ozs. onions
- 2 teaspoons of powdered sweet paprika
- 1 teaspoon of caraway seeds
- 1 teaspoon of dried marjoram
- 1 teaspoon of black pepper
- ½ teaspoon of salt
- ½ teaspoon of garlic salt
- a sprinkling of cayenne pepper, if preferred very hot
- 1 beef stock cube
- 4 tablespoons of cooking oil
- 2 frankfurter sausages

Procedure:

Peel and dice the onion, and brown in the cooking oil in a saucepan. Pour in a pint of water and boil for 17 minutes. Remove from the heat then pour in a dash of cold water with the rest of the ingredients, except the potatoes and frankfurters.

Warning! Never put sweet paprika directly into hot oil, as this can make it taste very bitter!

Stir well. Add the potatoes and simmer for 40 minutes. Thicken the goulash with a little pre-mixed flour and water, or any suitable thickening agent,

Cut the frankfurters into small slices and drop them into the casserole. Stir well for 5 minutes.

Serving:

Serve with brown bread, or a Viennese white bread roll, and a glass of cold beer.

SCHWEINSGULASCH
[Hot and Spicy Pork Casserole]

Ingredients, serves 2:

    18 ozs. pork meat, cut into medium sized pieces
    7 ozs. onions
    2 teaspoons powdered sweet paprika
    a sprinkling of black pepper and salt
    a sprinkling of cayenne pepper, if preferred very hot!
    1 ham stock cube
    4 tablespoons of cooking oil

Procedure:
    Peel and dice the onion, and brown in the cooking oil in a saucepan. Pour in half a pint of water and boil for 17 minutes.

    Remove from the heat then pour in a dash of cold water with the rest of the ingredients, except the meat.

    Warning! Never put sweet paprika directly into hot oil, as this can make it taste very bitter!

    Stir well, then add the meat. Simmer for 1 hour.

    Goulash should be thickened by adding a little pre-mixed flour and water, or any suitable thickening agent.

Serving:
    This dish should be served in a ring of rice.

REISFLEISCH
[Viennese Spicy Rice]

Ingredients, serves 2:

- 14 ozs. pork meat, cut into medium sized pieces
- 7 ozs. onions
- 2 teaspoons of powdered sweet paprika
- a sprinkling of black pepper and salt
- 1 ham stock cube
- 4 tablespoons of cooking oil
- 7 ozs. rice
- 2 tablespoons of grated Parmesan cheese

Procedure:

Cook the rice in the usual way. Meanwhile, peel and dice the onions, and brown in the cooking oil in a saucepan. Pour in a pint of water and boil for 17 minutes. Remove from heat then add a dash of cold water with the rest of the ingredients, except the meat. Warning! Never put sweet paprika directly into hot oil, as this can make it taste very bitter!

Stir well, then add the meat. Simmer for 50 minutes. This dish should be thickened by adding a little pre-mixed flour and water, or any suitable thickening agent.

Mix together the meat and the cooked rice, stirring over the heat for a further 5 minutes.

Serving:

This dish should be served with the Parmesan cheese sprinkled over it. It will look very attractive on the plate if the mixture is moulded into nice shapes using a large coffee cup.

PAPRIKAHUHN
[Spicy Chicken Casserole]

Ingredients, serves 2:

    18 ozs. chicken meat, cut into medium sized pieces
    7 ozs. onions
    2 teaspoons powdered sweet paprika
    a sprinkling of black pepper and salt
    1 chicken stock cube
    4 tablespoons cooking oil
    4 tablespoons créme fraiche

Procedure:
    Peel and dice the onion, and brown in the cooking oil in a saucepan. Pour in half a pint of water and boil for 17 minutes. Remove from the heat then pour in a dash of cold water with the rest of the ingredients, except the meat and créme fraiche.

    Warning! Never put sweet paprika directly into hot oil, as this can make it taste very bitter!

    Stir well, then add the meat. Simmer for 50 mins.

    This dish should be thickened by adding a little pre-mixed flour and water, or any suitable thickening agent.

    Remove from the heat and stir in the créme fraiche.

Serving:
    This dish should be served in a ring of rice.

FLEISCHPALATSCHINKEN
[Eva's Meat Pancakes]

Ingredients, serves 2:
Pancakes:
- 1 egg
- 3½ ozs. plain flour
- ½ pint milk
- 1 tablespoon of chopped chives
- a sprinkling of salt
- cooking oil as required

Filling:
- 18 ozs. of corned beef
- 1 tin of sliced carrots
- 1 medium onion
- 1 beef stock cube
- 1 teaspoon of dried marjoram
- a sprinkling of salt and pepper
- a dash of Worcestershire sauce
- 2 tablespoons of vegetable oil

Procedure:
Mix all the pancake ingredients together in a suitable jug.
Heat some cooking oil in a frying pan and make the mixture into thin pancakes. Place them in a warm oven for use later.
Put a little more oil in the frying pan then slice and brown the onions. Add the rest of the filling ingredients and stir-fry them for about 10 minutes. Fill the warm pancakes with the hot mixture, ready to serve.

Serving:
Sprinkle some Parmesan cheese over them and serve immediately.

GEBRATENE ENTE
[Roast Duck]

Ingredients, serves 4:

- 1 large duck, without giblets
- a sprinkling of dried thyme
- 1 tablespoon of marjoram
- 1 chicken stock cube
- ½ cup water
- 2 peeled oranges.
- 1 teaspoon of salt

Procedure:

Wash and dry the duck. Rub inside and all over it with the salt, thyme, and marjoram. Stuff with the oranges.

Heat up the water in a baking tray and crush in the chicken stock to later become the gravy. Place the duck in the tray, upside down.

Roast in a pre-heated oven to 395°F (200°C) for 1 hour and 45 minutes, basting occasionally with the gravy, turning the duck over half way through.

Place the duck on a serving plate. Take off the fat from the top of the gravy, then thicken the gravy with a little flour and water mixture, or any other preferred thickening agent.

Serving:

This dish should be served with potato dumplings and red cabbage, or with sauerkraut.
See the Soups and Savoury Dishes section.

FLEISCHTORTE
[Eva's Meat And Pancake Tart]

Ingredients, serves 4:
Pancakes:
- 1 egg
- 3½ ozs. plain flour
- ½ pint milk
- a sprinkling of salt
- 2 tablespoons of chopped chives
- cooking oil as required

Filling:
- 35 ozs. of corned beef
- 1 tin of sliced carrots
- 2 medium onions
- 1 beef stock cube
- 1 teaspoon of dried marjoram
- a sprinkling of salt and pepper
- a dash of Worcestershire sauce
- 2 tablespoons of vegetable oil

Topping:
- 1 green pepper
- 3½ ozs. grated cheese, (Cheddar or as preferred)

Procedure:

Mix the pancake ingredients together in a suitable jug.

Heat some cooking oil in a frying pan and make the mixture into about 6 thin pancakes. Put in a warm oven for later use.

Put a little more oil in the frying pan then slice and brown the onions. Put in the rest of the filling ingredients and stir-fry them for about 10 minutes.

Grease a round cake tin, preferably one with a

removable base. Next, place the first pancake into it, followed by a layer of the meat mixture.

Repeat the procedure for each pancake, but without any mixture on the last one.

Cut the pepper into thin slices and place them on top, followed by the grated cheese.

Bake in the oven at 360°F (180°C) for 45 minutes.

Serving:
    Best with a salad. See later in the next section.

FLEISCHKNÖDEL
[Meat Dumplings]

Ingredients, serves 2:
Dumplings:
- 18 ozs. potatoes
- 2 ozs. potato flour
- 2 ozs. semolina
- 1 small egg
- a sprinkling of salt

Filling:
- 18 ozs. corned beef
- 3½ ozs. diced bacon
- 1 medium sized onion
- 2 tablespoons of vegetable oil
- a sprinkling of marjoram and black pepper to taste

Procedure:

Cook the potatoes in their skins and peel them as in the recipe on page 66. While still hot squeeze the potato into a bowl, preferably using a potato press. Pour in the rest of the ingredients and mix into a pastry. Leave to stand for 15 minutes.

Meanwhile, heat the oil in a frying pan. Peel and slice the onion and glaze in the oil. Add the corned beef and seasoning, then fry for about 10 minutes. Half fill a large saucepan with salted water and bring to the boil. Separate 4 pieces of the pastry mixture on to a pastry board. Pick up a piece and flatten it in your hand. Spoon some meat mixture into its centre.

Fold and roll the pastry around the meat to hide it then repeat the process to make 4 dumplings. Drop them into the boiling water and simmer for 18 mins.

Serving:

Best served with sauerkraut or rotkraut. See the next section.

Vegetables & other SideDishes

NOTES

VEGETABLES AND OTHER SIDE DISHES

In Austria, we serve salads separately on a side plate, with the dressing already mixed in.

We make all kinds of salads, each in a different bowl, such as lettuce salad, tomato salad, potato salad, and so on. When we serve a meal, we ask guests which selections of salad they prefer. We then place their choices together on the side plate.

I personally make up my special salad dressing each week and keep it ready for use in the refrigerator.

Olive oil is best in salad dressing, but any other vegetable oil can be used if preferred.

For potato or French bean salads, the dressing is used to pickle the ingredients, so they are left for at least an hour to soak before use.

Vegetables, potatoes, and dumplings are always served on the main plate.

Potatoes are boiled in their skins and then peeled while still hot, using a fork and a knife. They are not usually roasted in the English way, but sliced and fried to make them crispy.

We serve vegetables, such as peas, carrots, and green beans,
cooked first and then enhanced with a special white sauce.

SAUERKRAUT
[Sweet and Sour White Cabbage]

Ingredients, serves 4:

    18 ozs. of pre-prepared sauerkraut
    1 teaspoon of caraway seeds
    1 vegetable stock cube
    2 tablespoons of plain flour
    2 tablespoons of honey
    1 medium sized apple
      a sprinkling of pepper

Procedure:

    Put the sauerkraut in a colander and gently rinse off the surplus liquid. Pour 1/2 pint of water into a saucepan.

    Add the sauerkraut, the vegetable stock cube and the caraway seeds. Boil the mixture for about 30 minutes, or until it is tender.

    Sprinkle on the flour, and stir it in, then boil for another 2 minutes. Add the honey and the pepper.

    Peel and grate the apple then add it to the mixture.

    Remove from the heat, it is now ready to serve.

    The finished sauerkraut, or any of it left over, can be deep frozen ready for use another day.

Serving:

    Serve hot with pork roast, (see page 30), or sliced and fried black pudding, or boiled smoked ham, or a boiled bacon joint.

ROTKRAUT
[Sweet and Sour Red Cabbage]

Ingredients, serves 4:

    18 ozs. of red cabbage
    1 medium sized cooking apple
    1 oz caster sugar
    1 oz plain flour
    ½ pint of red wine
    1 tablespoon of vinegar
    1 tablespoon of lemon juice
    1 vegetable stock cube
    a sprinkling of salt and pepper
    2 tablespoons of cooking oil

Procedure:
    Remove the centre stalk from the cabbage then slice up the rest thinly into a bowl. Pour the vinegar and lemon juice over the cabbage and leave to soak for about 15 minutes. Meanwhile, brown the sugar in the cooking oil in a saucepan.

    Add ½ cup of water, then the cabbage, the vegetable stock, and the salt and pepper and cook for about 30 minutes.

    Peel and grate the apple, and add it to the saucepan. Cook for another 30 minutes. Sprinkle over the flour and pour in the wine. Heat gently for 2 minutes.

Serving:
    Best served with any roast meat dish as an alternative to sauerkraut.

EINBRENN
[Special White Sauce for Vegetables]

When we cook runner beans, carrots, cabbage and peas, as well as leafy vegetables, we always serve them in this sauce. Vegetables cooked in the usual English way would only be served with grilled meat.

Ingredients:

    ½ cup vegetable oil
    1½ ozs. plain flour
    ¼ cup cold water

Procedure:

    Heat the oil in a frying pan, then add and lightly brown the flour.

    Remove from the heat and pour in the cold water. Stir briskly until the sauce thickens.

    Put to one side, ready for use with the vegetable recipes that follow.

FISOLEN ODER GRÜNE BOHNEN
[Creamed French or Runner Beans]

This side dish needs the white sauce recipe on page 54.

Ingredients, serves 2:

>7 ozs. beans
>½ cube of vegetable stock
>1¼ cups cold water (maximum)
>2 tablespoons of chopped dill
>2 tablespoons of créme fraiche
>a sprinkling of salt and pepper to taste

Procedure:
>Have the white sauce ready in a suitable saucepan. Pour the water into another saucepan. Add the vegetable stock cube and bring to the boil.
>
>Top and tail the beans. Cut into ½ inch long slices and put them into the saucepan of boiling water to simmer for about 30 minutes or until tender.
>
>Drain off and keep by, about half the cooking water. Tip the rest with the beans into the white sauce. Stir well and heat gently, adding the dill, salt and pepper. If necessary, add some of the drained cooking water until the mixture becomes smooth and creamy.
>
>>Remove from the heat and add the créme fraiche. Stir well, ready for use.

Serving:
>Good with all kinds of grilled or roast meat, sausages and crispy fried potatoes.,

KOHLRÜBEN MIT ERBSEN
[Creamed Kohlrabi with Peas]

This side dish needs the white sauce recipe on page 54.

Ingredients, serves 2:

    1 whole kohlrabi
    7 ozs. shelled garden peas
    ½ cube of vegetable stock
    1¼ cups cold water
    2 tablespoons of parsley
    2 tablespoons of créme fraiche
    a sprinkling of salt and pepper to taste

Procedure:
    Have the white sauce ready in a suitable saucepan. Pour the water into another saucepan and add the vegetable stock cube. Bring to the boil.

    Peel and cut the kohlrabi into small cubes and drop them in the saucepan of water to simmer for about 20 minutes. Add the peas and simmer for 10 more minutes.

    Drain off, and keep for later use, about half the cooking water. Tip the rest, with the vegetables, into the white sauce. Stir well and heat gently, adding the parsley, salt and pepper. Pour in enough of the drained cooking water, and keep stirring, until the mixture becomes smooth and creamy. Remove from the heat and add the créme fraiche.
    Stir well, ready for use.

Serving:
    Good with all kinds of grilled or roast meat, sausages and crispy fried potatoes.,

SPINAT
[Creamed Spinach]

This side dish needs the white sauce recipe on page 54.

Ingredients, serves 2:

    7 ozs. spinach leaves
    1 clove of garlic (optional)
    ½ cube of vegetable stock
    1 egg
    1¼ cups cold water (maximum)
    a sprinkling of salt and pepper

Procedure:
    Have the white sauce ready in a suitable saucepan.

    Pour the water into another saucepan. Add the garlic and vegetable stock cube and bring to the boil. Put in the spinach and simmer for 10 minutes. Take out the spinach and garlic, with a large fork, and put them in a blender. Keep the cooking water to one side for later use.

    Blend for 2 seconds at low speed with 2 tablespoons of the cooking water. Empty the spinach mixture into the saucepan of white sauce and heat gently, stirring in more and more of the cooking water, until the spinach becomes smooth and creamy. Remove from the heat and sprinkle in the salt and pepper.

    Briskly stir in the egg.

Serving:
    Good with sausages, or a fried egg and crispy fried potatoes.

KOHL
[Creamed Cabbage]

This side dish needs the white sauce recipe on page 54.

Ingredients, serves 2:
- 7 ozs. cabbage leaves
- 1 large potato
- 1 clove of garlic (optional)
- ½ cube of vegetable stock
- 1¼ cups cold water (maximum)
- 1 teaspoon of caraway seeds
- a sprinkling of salt and pepper

Procedure:

Have the white sauce ready in a suitable saucepan. Pour the water into another saucepan. Add garlic, the vegetable stock cube, and the caraway seeds, then bring to the boil. Peel and slice the potato, then add it with the cabbage and simmer for about 30 minutes.

Take out the cabbage, potato and garlic, with a large fork, and put them in a blender. Keep the cooking water to one side for later use.

Blend for 2 seconds at low speed with 2 tablespoons of the cooking water. Empty the mixture into the saucepan of white sauce and heat gently, stirring in more and more cooking water, until the mixture becomes smooth and creamy. Remove from the heat, sprinkle in the salt and pepper.

Serving:

Good with all kinds of sausages and crispy fried potatoes.

EVA'S SALATMARINADE
[Eva's Special Salad Dressing]

Ingredients, for 1/2 pint

> ½ cup cider vinegar, or any other kind as preferred
> ½ cup water
> 6 teaspoons of caster sugar, or 6 sweetener tablets, if preferred
> ½ teaspoon of garlic salt
> ½ teaspoon of dried marjoram
> a sprinkling of thyme
> a sprinkling of black pepper
> a dash of Worcestershire sauce

Procedure:

> Stir the ingredients together, with a fork, continuously for about a minute, then pour the dressing into a suitable bottle having a good stopper.
>
> Store, preferably in the refrigerator, for daily use, together with some virgin olive, as preferred, and described in the following recipes.

TOMATENSALAT
[Tomato Salad]

Ingredients, serves 2:

- 4 medium tomatoes
- 1 small onion
- 2 tablespoons of olive oil
- ½ cup pre-prepared salad dressing

Procedure:
Slice the tomatoes and place them in a salad bowl. Peel and slice the onion and add to the bowl. Pour on the dressing, followed by the oil. Mix together, ready to serve.

FISOLENSALAT
[French Bean Salad]

Ingredients, serves 2:

- 7 ozs. stringless French beans
- 1 small onion
- 2 tablespoons of olive oil
- ½ cup pre-prepared salad dressing

Procedure:
Top and tail the beans, and cut them in halves. Boil until tender. Drain off the water and place the beans, still hot, into a salad bowl. Peel and slice the onion and place on top of the beans. Pour on the dressing and leave for an hour to cool.

Finally pour on the olive oil. Mix together, ready to serve.

GRÜNER SALAT
[Lettuce Salad]

Ingredients, serves 2:

½ medium lettuce, can be Iceberg, or 2 Little Gems, or as preferred
1 tablespoon of chopped chives (optional)
2 tablespoons of olive oil
½ cup pre-prepared salad dressing

Procedure:
Slice the lettuce and place in a salad bowl.
Sprinkle over the chives.
Pour on the dressing, and mix well together.
Finally, pour on the oil and mix thoroughly together, ready to serve immediately.

WEISSER BOHNENSALAT
[White (Butter) Bean Salad]

Ingredients, serves 2:

½ pint canned butter beans
1 small onion
2 tablespoons of olive oil
½ cup pre-prepared salad dressing

Procedure:
Drain off the water from the beans and place them into a salad bowl. Peel and
slice the onion and place on top of the beans.
Pour on the dressing and mix well together.
Finally pour on the olive oil and mix together, ready to serve.

GURKENSALAT
[Cucumber Salad]

Ingredients, serves 2:
- ½ medium cucumber
- 1 teaspoon of crushed garlic (optional)
- 2 tablespoons of olive oil
- ½ cup pre-prepared salad dressing
- a sprinkling of salt to taste

Procedure:

Peel and thinly slice the cucumber on to a dry cloth. Sprinkle over the salt to extract the water, and press it out with one end of the cloth. Place the cucumber in a salad bowl with the garlic and the dressing, and mix well together.

Pour on the oil and mix thoroughly together. Leave for 30 minutes, ready to serve.

GURKENSALAT IN RAHM
[Creamed Cucumber Salad]

Ingredients, serves 2:
- ½ medium cucumber
- 4 tablespoons soured cream or créme fraiche
- ½ teaspoon of salt
- a generous sprinkling of black pepper
- a tablespoon of chopped chives

Procedure:

Prepare the cucumber as for the above recipe.

Place the dried cucumber, with the rest of the ingredients, into a salad bowl and mix well together, ready to serve immediately.

KARTOFFELSALAT
[Potato Salad]

Ingredients, serves 2:
- 2 large potatoes
- 1 small onion
- ½ cup (maximum) cider vinegar, or other as preferred
- ½ pint water
- ½ teaspoon of salt
- 2 tablespoons of sugar
- 2 tablespoons of vegetable oil

Procedure:
Mix together the vinegar, water, salt and sugar into a salad bowl. Boil the potatoes, then while still hot, peel and slice them into the bowl. Peel and slice the onion and place over the potatoes. Pour on the oil. Allow to cool, ready to serve.

KARTOFFELSALAT IN MAYONNAISE
[Potato and Mayonnaise Salad]

Ingredients, serves 2:
- 2 large potatoes
- 9 ozs. mayonnaise (can be low fat)
- a sprinkling of salt
- 1 generous sprinkling of black pepper
- 1 teaspoon of lemon juice
- 1 tablespoon of French mustard
- 1 tablespoon of caster sugar

Procedure:
Pour the mayonnaise and the rest of the ingredients, except the potato, into a salad bowl and mix well. Boil and peel the potatoes and slice them, still hot into the bowl. Mix everything well together and leave to cool, ready to serve.

APFELKREN
[Apple and Horseradish Sauce]

Ingredients:
- 3½ ozs. creamed horseradish
- 2 large sweet apples
- juice of 1 lemon
- 2 tablespoons of honey

Procedure:
Peel, and chop the apples and mix together with the rest of the ingredients.

Serving:
Excellent with cold Roast Beef, or boiled Gammon.

SEMMELKREN
[Bread and Horseradish Sauce]

Ingredients:
- 3 Viennese, or French, bread rolls
- ½ beef stock cube
- ½ cup single cream
- 2 tablespoons of horseradish sauce
- 1 teaspoon of sugar
- ¾ ozs. salted butter
- a dash of Worcestershire sauce
- ½ cup hot water

Procedure:
Make a stock from the ½ beef cube and the water and let it cool. Remove and discard the crusts from the rolls and soak the remainder in the stock. Bring to the boil and stir the mixture into a smooth sauce. Remove from the heat and add the single cream, horseradish sauce, sugar and the Worcestershire sauce. Finally add the butter and stir well.

Serving: Excellent with all kinds of cooked meat.

FLEISCHSALAT
[Meat Salad]

This dish can be made from all kinds of left over meat.

Ingredients, serves 2:
- 11 ozs. cooked meat
- 1 small onion
- ½ green pepper (optional)
- 2 tablespoons of olive oil
- ½ cup pre-prepared salad dressing

Procedure:
Slice the meat thinly and place it in a salad bowl. Peel and slice the onion and the green pepper and add to the bowl. Pour on the dressing, followed by the oil. Mix together, ready to serve.

HUHN IN MAYONNAISE SALAT
[Chicken in Mayonnaise Salad]

Ingredients, serves 2:
- 7 ozs. cooked chicken meat
- 9 ozs. cubed pineapple
- 3½ ozs. of seedless raisins, or sultanas
- 9 ozs. mayonnaise, can be low fat
- a sprinkling of salt and pepper to taste
- 1 teaspoon of lemon juice
- 1 tablespoon of French mustard
- 1 tablespoon of caster sugar

Procedure:
Pour the mayonnaise, pepper and salt, lemon juice, mustard and sugar in a bowl and mix well together. Slice the chicken meat and add it, with the raisins and the pineapple, into the mixture and stir well.

KARTOFFEL ALS BEILAGE
[Recipes for Potatoes as a Side Dish]

In Austria, potatoes are always served with their skins removed, even new potatoes. However, except for mashed potatoes, they are always cooked with the skins still on, after washing! For best results, when cooked, the hot water is drained off and the potatoes allowed to stand in the saucepan for about 5 minutes. Each potato is then picked up with a fork, in one hand. Then, using a sharp knife in the other hand, the skin is firmly removed. This can be done easier on a cutting board. Generally, 2 medium sized potatoes should be allowed per person.

GEKOCHTE KARTOFFEL
[Boiled Potatoes]

For goulash dishes, potatoes are served, directly after preparation as described above.

MITGEBRATENE KARTOFFEL
[Simple Fried Potatoes]

These are first prepared as above, then subsequently sliced and crispy fried in the same oil, for example, that which has been used to prepare a Wienerschnitzel dish. (see page 28)

GERÖSTETE KARTOFFEL
[Crispy Fried Potatoes]

For a more exotic recipe, brown some chopped onion in a frying pan first, then add the potatoes, cut into slices, with a sprinkling of salt and pepper. Fry everything long enough to give a really crispy texture to the potatoes.

PETERSILKARTOFFELN
[Parsley Potatoes]

Procedure:
Melt some salted butter in a suitable bowl, then add a sprinkling of powdered nutmeg, and chopped parsley. Mix together, then cut each potato in half and roll them in the mixture, ready to serve.

DILLKARTOFFELN
[Dill Potatoes]

Procedure:
Warm up ½ cup of soured cream, or créme fraiche, in a saucepan. Mix in a tablespoonful of chopped dill. Crumble in half a cube of vegetable stock, and a sprinkling of nutmeg powder. Cut each potato in half and roll them in the saucepan mixture, ready to serve.

KARTOFFELPÜREE
[Mashed Potatoes]

Ingredients, serves 4:
   8 medium sized potatoes
   4 tablespoons of salted butter
   a sprinkling of powdered nutmeg
   ½ pint hot milk

Procedure:
For this recipe, peel the potatoes first! Then cut them in half; never in smaller pieces as they may become too watery. Boil them in salty water until soft. Drain off the water, then add the butter. Sprinkle on the powdered nutmeg, then pour on the milk. Mash the potatoes until creamy.

Serving:
For extra enjoyment, try sprinkling some crispy fried onion rings over the mashed potato.

SEMMELKNÖDEL
[Viennese Bread Roll Dumplings]

The main ingredient for this dish is small cubes of bread cut up from Viennese Bread Rolls, which are then oven dried at 212°F (100°C) on a tray. In this condition they can be stored in an airtight container for use at any time when required.

Ingredients, serves 4:
- 4 Viennese bread rolls prepared as above
- 2 ozs. salted butter
- 1 tablespoon of chopped parsley
- 1 medium egg
- ½ pint milk
- 3 ozs. plain flour
- a sprinkling of salt

Procedure:

Brown the breadcrumbs, with the chopped parsley, in the butter. Pour the milk into a bowl with the egg and mix well. Tip in the breadcrumbs and sprinkle in the flour and salt. Mix well together. The mixture needs to be like a stiff pastry. If too wet, mix in some more flour. Leave to stand for about an hour.

Meanwhile, half fill a large saucepan with salted water and bring to the boil.

Before forming the dumplings, wet your hands in cold water. With the water boiling fast in the saucepan, shape the mixture into 8 balls and drop them slowly into the water, which must be kept boiling briskly. Boil for 15 minutes. Finally remove them, with a hand-strainer, on to a plate.

Serving:

Best with pork roast and sauerkraut. Any left over can be used for a vegetarian dish. See the next section.

KARTOFFELKNÖDEL
[Potato Dumplings]

Ingredients:

    18 ozs. of potatoes
    2 ozs. of potato flour
    2 ozs. semolina
    1 small egg
    a sprinkling of salt

Procedure:
    Cook the potatoes in their skins and peel them as in the recipe on page 66. While still hot, squeeze all the potatoes into a bowl, preferably using a potato press. Pour in the rest of the ingredients and mix into a pastry. Leave to stand for 15 minutes.

    Meanwhile, half fill a large saucepan with salted water and bring to the boil.

    Form 8 dumplings from the pastry mixture and drop them into the fast boiling water. Simmer for 15 minutes.

Serving:
    Best served with sauerkraut or rotkraut.
    See pages 52 and 53.

SERVIETTENKNÖDEL
[Dumplings Cooked in a Cloth]

The main ingredient for this dish is small cubes of bread cut up from Viennese Bread Rolls which are then oven dried at 212°F (100°C) on a tray. In this condition they can be stored in an airtight container for use at any time when required.

Ingredients, serves 4:
    4 Viennese bread rolls prepared as above
    2½ ozs. salted butter
    1 tablespoon of chopped parsley
    2 medium eggs
    ½ pint milk
    1 medium onion
      a sprinkling of salt
      a sprinkling of nutmeg

Procedure:
    Peel and finely chop the onion and glaze in oil. Place the eggs and milk in a bowl and stir well, then add the cubed bread, the onion, and the rest of the ingredients. Mix well and leave for 2 hours. Next, half fill a large saucepan with salted water and bring to the boil. Take a clean cloth and lay it down on a work surface. Place the dumpling mixture on it and roll it up in the cloth. Tie a string around each end making sure that everything is tight. Place the wrapped dumpling mixture in the boiling water and simmer for 45 minutes.

    When done, make sure your hands are protected from the heat, then place the wrapped mixture back on the work surface. Remove the cloth and cut the dumpling roll into slices about 2 cm thick, ready to serve.

Serving:
    Best with any game dish, such as venison.

Meat Free Dishes

NOTES

Introduction to MEAT FREE DISHES

In Austria, we serve many meals without meat. You will find some of them in the Side Dishes section, as well as the Sweet Dishes section.

Children especially enjoy meals of dumplings with a special tomato sauce, as well as just pancakes with a jam sauce.

KAROTTEN UND ERBSEN GEMÜSE
[Carrots and Peas]

Ingredients, serves 2:

    14 ozs. carrots
    7 ozs. shelled garden peas
    1 large onion
    ½ cube of vegetable stock
    4 tablespoons of cooking oil, or orange juice if preferred
    2 tablespoons of parsley
    2 tablespoons of créme fraiche
    a sprinkling of salt and pepper to taste

Procedure:
    Heat the oil in a saucepan. Peel and cut the onion and glaze it in the oil. Peel and thinly slice the carrots and add them, with the vegetable stock, salt and pepper. Fry gently with 2 tablespoons of water, or orange juice, for 30 minutes.

    Add the peas and the parsley. Cook for a further 10 minutes.

    Remove from the heat and add the créme fraiche. Stir well, ready for use.

Serving:
    Good with Kartoffelpuffer! See page 80.

KARFIOL MIT BUTTER UND BRÖSEL
[Cauliflower with Butter and Breadcrumbs]

Ingredients, serves 2:

    1 cauliflower
    9 ozs. breadcrumbs
    3½ ozs. salted butter
    a sprinkling of powdered nutmeg

Procedure:

    Cut off the florets (flower tops) of the cauliflower, (you can use the stalks as well if preferred), then boil them in salty water until tender.

    Meanwhile, melt the butter in a frying pan, put in the breadcrumbs and fry them until golden brown. and crunchy.

    Sprinkle on the nutmeg and mix well together.

    Drain the cauliflower florets and serve them immediately, with the breadcrumbs mixture tipped over them.

GERÖSTETE KNÖDEL
[Roasted Dumplings]

The main ingredient for this dish is the dumplings recipe in the Side Dishes section, page 68.

Ingredients, serves 2:

    4 pre-prepared dumplings
    3 medium sized eggs
    1 medium sized onion (optional)
    3 tablespoons of vegetable oil
    2 tablespoons of chopped chives (optional)
    a sprinkling of pepper and salt

Procedure:
    Peel and slice the onion.

    Heat the oil in a frying pan then add and brown the onion. Cut the dumplings in half then into smaller slices. Add them to the onion and fry until crispy brown on both sides.

    Meanwhile break and tip the eggs in a bowl and whisk well. Add the pepper and salt and pour the mixture over the dumplings.

    Stir continuously until the egg mixture is set.

Serving:
    Best with lettuce or tomato salad.
    See pages 59-61.

TOMATENSAUCE MIT KNÖDEL
[Special Tomato Sauce with Dumplings]

The main ingredient for this dish is the dumplings recipe in the Side Dishes section, page 68. It has a sweet and sour taste which children like very much.

Ingredients, serves 2:

- 2 pre-prepared dumplings
- 1 tin of thick, cream of tomato, soup
- 3 tablespoons of vegetable oil
- 2 tablespoons of plain flour
- 1 tablespoon of sugar
- a sprinkling of pepper

Procedure:

Heat the oil in a frying pan then add and brown the flour. Remove from the heat and pour in 2 tablespoons of cold water. Stir well then pour in the tomato soup with the sugar and pepper.

Cook for 5 minutes, stirring briskly.

Serving:

On individual plates of dumplings with the sauce poured over them. This sauce is also often served over potatoes or rice.

CHAMPIGNONSAUCE MIT KNÖDEL
[Mushroom Sauce with Dumplings]

The main ingredient for this dish is the dumplings recipe in the Side Dishes section, page 68.

Ingredients, serves 2:

- 2 pre-prepared dumplings
- 18 ozs. mushrooms
- 3 tablespoons of vegetable oil
- 1 tablespoon of plain flour
- ½ cup milk
- 1 small onion
- ½ vegetable stock cube
- 2 tablespoons of chopped parsley
- a sprinkling of pepper and salt

Procedure:

Heat the oil in a frying pan then peel, slice and glaze the onion.

Wash and slice the mushrooms and add to the onion. Fry gently for about 10 minutes.

Crumble and add the vegetable stock. Add the pepper and salt, and the parsley. Sprinkle on the flour then add the milk.

Stir continuously until the sauce thickens, ready to serve with the dumplings.

GEFÜLLTE MELANZANI
[Stuffed Aubergine]

Ingredients, serves 2:
- 1 aubergine (eggplant)
- 1 medium onion
- 3½ ozs. mushrooms
- 4 tablespoons of vegetable oil
- 1 tablespoon of breadcrumbs
- 1 tablespoon of chopped parsley
- 1 tablespoon of Parmesan cheese
- a sprinkling of salt and black pepper

Procedure:

On a work board, cut the aubergine in half lengthways. Score along the open sides with a knife, in both directions, producing crossways cuts.

Pour half the oil in a frying pan with the aubergine halves, open sides down. Fry until the open sides are brown, then place them on a cutting board. Pull out out the seeds sections with a spoon, ready for use. Put the rest of the oil in the frying pan and heat gently. Peel and slice the onion, and glaze in the oil. Chop the seeds sections into small slices, then wash and slice the mushrooms. Put everything in the frying pan with the parsley, salt and pepper, and fry for 10 minutes.

Remove from the heat. Sprinkle on the breadcrumbs and mix well together. Stuff the aubergines' shells with the mixture, then sprinkle on the cheese. Place them on an oven tray and bake for 35 mins at 395°F (200°C).

Serving:

With mashed potato. See page 67.

KARTOFFELPUFFER
[Puffed Potato Pancakes]

Ingredients, serves 4-6:
- 35 ozs. potatoes
- 1 egg
- 6 tablespoons plain flour
- 1 teaspoon of salt
- 1 teaspoon of finely chopped garlic
- a sprinkling of ground black pepper
- 1 teaspoon of dried marjoram

Procedure:
Peel the potatoes and grate them on to a dry cloth. Sprinkle on the salt and leave a while to be absorbed. Fold up the cloth around the potato strips and firmly squeeze out as much liquid as possible.

Take a large frying pan and pour in enough vegetable oil to just cover the base, then place it on the stove and begin to heat gently.

Pour the flour into a mixing bowl. Add the garlic, the pepper, and the marjoram.

Slide in the dried, grated potato, then the egg. Mix rapidly with a large wooden spoon. Part out the mixture into small separate sections. Remove each section and shape it, pressing down firmly, into pancakes on a lightly floured cutting board. When ready, place the pancakes into the heated frying pan.

Turn up the heat and fry each side quickly. Serve immediately.

Serving:
This simple, tasty, savoury dish is ideal as a snack or as a barbecue starter, or served with a vegetable dish.

KARTOFFELGULASCH
[Meat Free, Hot and Spicy Potato Casserole]

Ingredients, serves 2:

> 18 ozs. potatoes, cut into small pieces
> 14 ozs. onions
> 2 teaspoons of powdered sweet paprika
> 1 teaspoon of caraway seed
> 1 teaspoon of dried marjoram
> a sprinkling of black pepper and salt
> ½ teaspoon of garlic salt
> a dash of cayenne pepper, if wanted very hot
> 1 vegetable stock cube
> 4 tablespoons of cooking oil

Procedure:

> Peel and dice the onion, and brown in the cooking oil in a saucepan. Pour in one and three quarters cups of water and boil for 15 minutes.
>
> Remove from the heat then pour in a dash of cold water. Add the rest of the ingredients, except the potatoes.
>
> Warning! Never put sweet paprika directly into hot oil, as this can make it taste very bitter!
>
> Stir well, then add the potatoes. Simmer for 40 minutes.
>
> Thicken the goulash with a little pre-mixed flour and water, or any suitable thickening agent.

Serving:

> Serve with brown bread, or a Viennese white bread roll, and a glass of cold beer.

PANIERTER KARFIOL
[Cauliflower in Breadcrumbs]]

You could use raw mushrooms, cooked potatoes, cooked parsnips, or any other preferred vegetables for this dish.

Ingredients, serves 2:
- 1 cauliflower
- 1 vegetable stock cube
- 1 egg
- 6 tablespoons of plain flour, not self-raising
- 6 tablespoons of dried golden breadcrumbs
- a sprinkling of salt
- 1¼ cups cooking oil

Procedure:
> Make a stock with the vegetable cube and 1 pint of water. Cut off the florets (cauliflower tops) then boil them in the stock.
>
> Meanwhile, take 2 dinner plates and a large soup plate. Put the flour on the first dinner plate, breadcrumbs on the second. Break the egg into 1 tablespoon of water in the soup plate with the salt, and stir well together. When the cauliflower is ready, remove it from the stock and drain it. Dry each floret carefully on some kitchen paper. Next, dip them into the plate of flour then into the egg mixture. Finally, press them into the plate of breadcrumbs, making sure the coating is even all over.
>
> Rapidly heat up the oil in a suitable frying pan until very hot. Carefully place the florets into the hot oil and fry them until golden brown all over, turning them occasionally.

Serving: Best with sauce tartare.

Sweet Dishes & Desserts

NOTES

PALATSCHINKEN
[Basic Pancake Recipe]

Ingredients, serves 2:

    1 egg
    3½ ozs. plain flour
    ½ pint milk
    1 teaspoon of sugar
    a sprinkling of salt
    cooking oil as required

Procedure:
    Mix all the ingredients together in a suitable jug.

    Heat some cooking oil in a frying pan and make the mixture into thin pancakes. Serve as soon as possible!

Serving:
    In Austria, the most popular fillings for pancakes are strawberry or apricot jam, with powdered sugar sprinkled over them.

    My husband prefers lemon juice and sugar.

TOPFENPALATSCHINKEN
[Quark Cheese Pancakes]

Ingredients, serves 2:
Pancakes:
  1 egg
  3½ ozs. plain flour
  ½ cup milk
  1 teaspoon of sugar
  a sprinkling of salt
  cooking oil as required
Filling:
  8 ozs. of quark
  2 ozs. of unsalted butter
  3½ ozs. caster sugar
  3½ ozs. sultanas
  1 teaspoon of lemon zest
  2 eggs separated into yolks and whites
Topping:
  ½ cup milk
  ½ pint créme fraiche
  2 ozs. of caster sugar
  2 egg yolks
Procedure:
  Mix all the pancake ingredients together in a jug. Heat some cooking oil in a frying pan and make the mixture into thin pancakes. Leave to one side for use later. Mix all the filling ingredients together in a bowl, except the egg whites. Stiffen the egg whites, then carefully fold them into the filling mixture. Butter a baking dish, and place a pancake in it. Spoon on some of the filling mixture. Fold the pancake over. Repeat for the rest of the pancakes. Mix the topping ingredients and pour all over the pancakes to cover them. Bake for 35 minutes at about 350°F (180°C).
Serving:
  Best served with a vanilla sauce, (English custard is fine).

ÄPFEL IM SCHLAFROCK
[Apple in a Dressing Gown!]

Ingredients, serves 2:

    2 sweet apples
    1 egg
    ½ ozs. plain flour
    ¾ cup milk
    1 tablespoon of sugar
    cooking oil as required

Procedure:
    Peel and core the apples and slice them into rings.

    Mix the rest of the ingredients together in a large bowl.

    Heat some cooking oil in a frying pan.

    Drop the apple slices into the mixture to coat them then fry until the batter is browned.

Serving:
    Serve with powdered sugar sprinkled over them.

KAISERSCHMARREN
[Emperor's Cut Up Pancakes]

This recipe name came about because our old Emperor Franz Joseph had a very sweet tooth. He didn't want his pancakes served in the traditional way. He liked them thicker and broken up into small pieces.

Ingredients:
- 3 egg yolks
- 3 egg whites
- 12 ozs. self-raising flour
- ½ pint milk
- 1 tablespoon of sugar
- 3½ ozs. seedless raisins or sultanas
- 4 ozs. unsalted butter

Procedure:
Put the flour and milk in a bowl and mix together. Add egg yolks in turn, while mixing. Melt half the butter and pour it in with the sugar and the raisins.

Whisk the egg whites until stiff. Fold them carefully into the mixture. Warm a large rectangular baking dish and gently melt the butter into it. Pour in the mixture, then bake at 350°F (180°C) for about 30 minutes or until the top has turned golden brown and crispy.

Remove the dish from the oven and turn the mixture over with a spatula. Put it back in the oven and bake for about 10 more minutes until the other side is golden brown and crispy.

Remove from the oven and with two forks, break up the mixture into small pieces.

Serving:
Best hot, with extra sugar and cold tinned fruit.

SCHEITERHAUFEN
[Apple Layer Cake]

Ingredients, serves 2:

    4 currant buns, or 2 teacakes
    4 sweet apples
    ½ pint milk
    2 egg yolks
    1 teaspoon of powdered cinnamon
    3½ ozs. sugar
    3½ ozs. seedless raisins, or sultanas
    3½ ozs. unsalted butter

Topping:
    2 egg whites
    3½ ozs. sugar
    3½ ozs. chopped walnuts

Procedure:

    Mix together the milk, the egg yolks, and the sugar, in a bowl. Cut the buns into small slices. Peel and slice the apples.

    Butter a small round soufflé dish. Place one layer of sliced bun in first, followed by slices of apple and so on. Make the last layer from the apples. Sprinkle the raisins and cinnamon over the top then pour on the milk mixture. Leave to soak for about 15 mins.

    Bake for 40 mins at 350°F (180°C). Meanwhile, whisk the egg whites with the sugar and walnuts until stiff.

    When done, remove the cake from the oven and spread the topping over it. Put back in the oven for about 5 minutes to set and brown the topping.

MARILLENKNÖDEL
[Apricot Dumplings]

Ingredients, serves 2:
Dumplings:
- 6 fresh apricots
- 6 knobs of sugar
- 9 ozs. quark
- 5½ ozs. plain flour
- 1 egg
- 2 ozs. unsalted butter

Coating:
- 6 digestive biscuits, finely crushed
- 3½ ozs. unsalted butter

Procedure:
Carefully remove the stones from the apricots, and replace them with the knobs of sugar. Cream the butter in a pastry bowl and then stir in the egg.
Add the quark and the flour and mix well to a pastry mixture. Leave to stand for 15 minutes. Meanwhile, half fill a large saucepan with water and bring it to the boil.

Separate out 6 pieces of the pastry mixture on to a pastry board. Pick up a piece and flatten it in your hand, then place an apricot into its centre. Fold and roll the pastry around the apricot to hide it, then repeat the process to make 6 dumplings. Drop them into the boiling water and simmer for 18 mins. Meanwhile, brown the biscuit crumbs in the rest of the butter. Roll each dumpling in the mixture, ready to serve.

Serving:
Serve with powdered sugar and the rest of the topping mixture sprinkled over the dumplings.

Cakes & Biscuits

NOTES

APFELKUCHEN
[Mother's Apple Turnover]

Ingredients:
Pastry:
- 11 ozs. of self-raising flour
- 3½ ozs. of slightly salted butter
- ½ cup of milk

Filling:
- 2 large cooking apples
- 1 tablespoon of brown sugar
- 1 teaspoon of powdered cinnamon
- 3½ ozs. of seedless raisins

Procedure:
Peel the apples and remove the cores. Cut into thin slices. Place the slices into a saucepan on the stove and blanch them, (part cook gently for about 5 minutes, with just a small amount of boiling water). Remove from the heat and strain off the water. Place all the pastry ingredients in a mixing bowl and gently blend together. Put the pastry into the refrigerator for 15 minutes.

Remove the mixture from the mixing bowl and then place it on to a floured pastry board. Roll it out to a square, about 16 inches a side. Place the part cooked apples on top and sprinkle over with the brown sugar, raisins and cinnamon. Lift up one edge and fold it over to the centre.

Lift up the other edge and fold it across the centre to form the turnover. Carefully slide the completed roll on to a buttered baking tray. Brush on some milk, then bake in a pre-heated oven at about 390°F (200°C) for 40 minutes.

Serving: When nicely browned, remove from the oven and sprinkle some powdered sugar over it. This dish is best served cold or just slightly warm.

WIENER APFELSTRUDEL
[Viennese Apple Pastry]

Ingredients:
   1 pack of frozen filo pastry
   3½ ozs. unsalted butter, or vegetable oil
   2 cooking apples
   3½ ozs. caster sugar
   3½ ozs. sultanas
   3½ ozs. breadcrumbs
   1 teaspoon of powdered cinnamon

Procedure:
   Defrost the filo pastry as recommended on the package.

   Heat 3 ozs. of butter and drop in the breadcrumbs. Stir them around until golden brown. Peel and core the apples and cut them into small slices. Melt the remaining butter ready to brush on the pastry.

   Now dampen a clean cloth or tea-towel and lay it flat on the working surface. Unwrap the filo pastry and build up 2 overlapping layers, about 12 ins by 12 ins square, over the cloth, brushing over each layer with melted butter as they build up. Keep any left over filo pastry in a plastic bag, but for use the following day at the latest.

   Sprinkle breadcrumbs over the pastry, leaving a border about an inch wide, all around the edge. Place on the apple pieces, followed by the cinnamon, the sugar and finally the sultanas, all spread evenly on the breadcrumbs.

   Take one side of the cloth and use it to fold over the uncovered edge of the pastry. Repeat the procedure for the the opposite side only. Take one of the other edges of the cloth and bring it over and over, so that the strudel folds up like a Swiss roll.

Butter a baking tray and carefully, using the damp cloth, roll the strudel over on to it.

Bake at 390°F (200°C) for 40 minutes.

Serving:
Dust over first with powdered sugar.

Note:
Blackcurrants, blueberries, or blackberries can replace apples in this recipe.

SCHOKOLADEKUCHEN
[Eva's Special Chocolate Cake]

Ingredients:
Cake:
- ½ cup water
- ½ cup vegetable oil
- 3 eggs
- 7 ozs. caster sugar
- 3½ ozs. drinking chocolate powder
- 5½ ozs. self-raising flour
- 1½ teaspoons of baking powder
- 3 drops of almond essence

Icing:
- 8 digestive biscuits, or similar crunchy type
- 5 tablespoons of rum, or brandy
- 2 tablespoons of strawberry jelly preserve

Procedure:

Blend the icing ingredients in a bowl, making sure the biscuits break down and soak up the liquid. Keep for use when the cake is baked. Pre-heat the oven to 212°F (100°C). Start up your mixer at fast speed. Put in the water and the vegetable oil. Break one egg after the other into the liquid. Add the caster sugar and almond essence and leave running for 5 minutes. Switch to half-speed and put in the chocolate powder. Stir the baking powder into the flour, then pour it into the mixer. Leave it running for about 2 minutes then pour the liquid mixture into a non-stick round baking tin, the type with a removable base is best. Place in the centre of the lower shelf of the oven, and up temperature to 350°F (180°C).

Bake for 45 minutes, without opening the oven door. Allow the cake to cool to cool then spread the icing mixture over it.

Serving:
Serve with whipped cream.

KIRSCHENKUCHEN
[Cherry Cake]

Ingredients:
Cake:
- 3 egg yolks
- 7 ozs. unsalted butter
- 7 ozs. caster sugar
- 7 ozs. self-raising flour
- 3 egg whites

Topping:
- 10 ozs. stoned fresh cherries

Procedure:

Whip the egg whites in a bowl until stiff. Put the butter, egg yolks, and sugar in a separate bowl and mix thoroughly. Add the flour and mix well. Finally blend in the egg white.

Butter a long, rectangular baking tin and then sprinkle it with flour. Pour in the cake mixture.

Drop the cherries evenly over the mixture.

Bake at 350°F (180°C) for about 45 minutes.

MARILLENKUCHEN
[Apricot Cake]

Ingredients:
- 3½ ozs. water
- 3½ ozs. vegetable oil
- 3 eggs
- 7 ozs. caster sugar
- 9 ozs. self-raising flour
- 1½ teaspoons of baking powder
- 3 drops of lemon essence
- 7 fresh apricots

Procedure:

Stone the apricots and cut them into little slices.

Pre-heat the oven to 212°F (100°C).

Start up the mixer at fast speed. Put in the water and the vegetable oil, then break one egg after the other into the liquid.

Add the caster sugar and the lemon essence and leave running for 5 minutes. Switch the machine to half-speed. Stir the baking powder into the flour, then pour it into the machine. Leave running for 2 minutes.

Butter a deep baking tray and sprinkle it all over with self-raising flour. Pour the mixture, which will still be liquid, into the tray. Drop the apricot pieces in evenly over the mixture.

Place on the lower shelf of the oven, positioned centrally, and increase the temperature to 350°F (180°C). Bake for 30 minutes, without opening the oven door.

When the cake is done and while still hot, sprinkle some powdered sugar over it.

FRUCHTKUCHEN
[Fruit Cake]

Ingredients:
- 4 egg yolks
- 3½ ozs. unsalted butter
- 7 ozs. caster sugar
- 7 ozs. self-raising flour
- 4 egg whites
- 3½ ozs. walnut pieces
- 2 ozs. candied orange peel
- 2 ozs. candied glacé mixed fruit
- 2 ozs. seedless raisins
- 2 ozs. plain chocolate bar

Procedure:

Whip the egg white in a bowl until stiff.

Cut the fruit mixture and chocolate bar into small pieces and put to one side. Put the butter, egg yolks, and sugar in a separate bowl and mix thoroughly. Add the flour and mix well.

Mix in the fruit and chocolate and then finally fold in the egg white.

Butter a long, rectangular, baking tin and sprinkle it with flour. Pour in the cake mixture.

Bake at 350°F (180°C) for about 40 minutes.

BISKOTTENTORTE
[Custard and Sponge Fingers Cake]

Ingredients:
- 2 packets of sponge finger biscuits
- 1½ pints milk
- 2 tablespoons custard powder
- 3 tablespoons sugar
- 5 drops of almond essence
- 1 cup of fruit jelly preserve
- 1 bar of icing chocolate

Procedure:

Make up the custard using only 1 pint of milk. Put the rest of the milk into a small bowl and stir in the almond essence.

Dip each sponge finger into the liquid and lay them one after the other in an 8 inches diameter round baking tin, covering the base first. Spread all the fruit jelly preserve as a second layer over the sponge fingers.

Add another layer of sponge fingers, each first dipped into the milk liquid. Pour over a layer of the custard, then another layer of liquid soaked biscuits. Continue to build up the cake leaving the final layer as sponge fingers only. Place the cake in the refrigerator for 24 hours.

Remove the cake from its tin by inverting it over a plate or tray. Melt the icing chocolate, in accordance with the instructions on the packet, and spread it over the cake.

Serving:

Serve with a generous helping of whipped cream.

NUSSKEKS
[Nut Biscuits]

Ingredients:

    1 egg
    3½ ozs. unsalted Butter
    11 oz caster sugar
    9 ozs. plain flour
    3½ ozs. ground walnuts

Procedure:

    Mix all the ingredients together into a smooth pastry. Place in the refrigerator for 30 minutes.

    Remove the mixture and roll it out to a biscuit thickness of about ¼ inch maximum.

    Cut out biscuit shapes with any suitable former, and place them on a buttered baking tray. Leave enough space between them to prevent sticking together.

    Put the tray into a pre-heated oven at 350°F (180°C) for about 12 to 15 minutes.

HUSARENBUSSERLN
[Hussar Kisses!]

Ingredients:
Biscuit:
    1 egg
    5½ ozs. unsalted butter
    ¼ oz caster sugar
    12½ ozs. plain flour
    2½ ozs. ground walnuts
    1 teaspoon of cinnamon powder
      zest (tiny skin strips) from half a lemon

Topping:
    Strawberry jam as required

Procedure:
Mix all the biscuit ingredients together into a smooth pastry. Place in the refrigerator for 30 minutes.

Put the mixture on to a pastry board and form into balls about 1 inch diameter. Place the balls on a buttered baking tray, with enough space between to prevent them sticking together.

Put the tray into a pre-heated oven at 350°F (180°C) for 5 minutes to part bake them.

Remove the tray from the oven. In turn press each ball with the handle end of a small wooden spoon to form a little depression. Spoon some jam into each depression.

Finally, put the tray back in the heated oven for about another 8 to 10 minutes

MARZIPANPILZE
[Marzipan Mushrooms]

Ingredients:

11½ ozs. caster sugar
4 ozs. ground almonds
4 ozs. milk chocolate bar

Procedure:
Mix the sugar and almonds together into a smooth paste.

Separate the paste into two parts and put one of them aside to be the 'white' stalks.

Melt 3½ ozs. of the chocolate bar in a bowl over some hot water. Pour and mix it into the other part of the paste. This will be for the 'brown' heads.

From the brown paste, form about twenty small balls on a pastry board. Do the same with the white paste.

Gently press each brown ball into a mushroom head shape. Gently roll each white ball into a stubby mushroom stalk shape.

Melt the rest of the chocolate bar and use it to cement each stalk into a mushroom head.

RUMKUGELN
[Rum Balls]

Ingredients:

    3½ ozs. ground walnuts
    3½ ozs. caster sugar
    3½ ozs. bar of milk chocolate
    2 tablespoons of brown rum (or can be brandy)
    2 drops of almond essence

Decoration:

    3½ ozs. peeled hazelnuts

Procedure:

    Put the ingredients into a bowl and mix into a smooth pastry. Form into ¾ inch diameter balls on a tray. Decorate by pushing hazelnut into each ball.

    Store the tray in a cool, dry, place for about 2 weeks to dry.

Serving:

    These 'sweets' make an attractive decoration when served together with a big plate of Christmas biscuits. See pages 101, 102, and 106.

TOPFENTEIGPOLSTERLN
[Quark Pastry Pillows]

Ingredients:
Pastry:
- 9 ozs. quark
- 7 ozs. unsalted butter
- 9 ozs. plain flour

Filling:
- 7 ozs. strawberry jam

Procedure:
Mix the pastry ingredients together into a smooth pastry.

Leave to stand for about 30 minutes.

Roll the pastry out on a floured board and cut it out into small squares about 2 inches wide.

Spread some jam into the centre of the first square and then fold over the pastry, corner to corner. Press along each side to seal in the jam.

Bake in the oven at 350°F (180°C) for about 20 minutes.

Serving:
Serve with powdered sugar sprinkled over them.

VANILLEKIPFERLN
[Vanilla Crescent Biscuits]

Ingredients:

    3½ ozs. unsalted butter
    2 ozs. ground almonds
    1 oz. caster sugar
    5½ ozs. plain flour
    7 ozs. vanilla sugar

Procedure:

    Pour the vanilla sugar into a bowl for use later. Mix up the rest of the ingredients into a pastry and place it into the refrigerator for 15 minutes.

    Place the mixture on to a floured pastry tray. Form it out with your fingers into a long, round roll of about ½ inch diameter.

    Cut the roll into 2 inches long sections. Form each section into a crescent moon shape, and place them on to a buttered baking tray. Put the tray in the oven at 300°F (150°C) and bake for about 18 minutes, but do not let them turn brown.

    Remove the biscuits, and while still hot, drop them carefully into the bowl of vanilla sugar and coat them all over, one by one.

Serving:

    These very tempting biscuits are a Viennese Christmas speciality!

NOTES

NOTES

NOTES

"Good Cooking …!

… and you might like to see my website?"

www.evaethorne.webs.com

Eva Thorne

Etcetera Press